The Fruit of the Spirit

Developing powerful attributes that
help kids be more like Jesus!

Grades 1–3

by

Thomas C. Ewald

Carson-Dellosa Christian Publishing

Greensboro, North Carolina

Editor ....Carol Layton

Layout Design ....Mark Conrad

Inside Illustrations ....Joni Oeltjenbruns

Cover Design ....Peggy Jackson

Photos..................................www.comstock.com

© Rubberball Productions

Scripture taken from the HOLY BIBLE, NEW INTERNATIONAL VERSION Copyright © 1973, 1978, 1984 International Bible Society. Used by permission of Zondervan Bible Publishers.

ISBN 0-88724-139-5

Table of Contents

Introduction

The fruit of the Holy Spirit is more than just a group of character traits that make us more pleasant to be around. When we accept Jesus as our Lord and Savior, God plants seeds of Himself in us so that as they grow, others see Him in our lives. When yielded to, these seeds mature and become powerful forces that cause us to be all that God created us to be.

The activities in this book will teach children to nurture the fruit of the Spirit by exercising it—by choosing to respond in love for example, rather than reacting in jealousy or pride. As we learn to exercise the fruit that He has placed in us, it matures—it becomes stronger and sweeter—and so do we!

While the *gifts* of the Spirit are given to Christians in differing measures (1 Corinthians 12:4–11), the fruit of the Spirit is given alike to all believers. It is up to the believer to choose to yield to the Holy Spirit so that the fruit can mature and become manifested in his life.

Galatians 6:7–9 tells us how the fruit of the Spirit develops in us:

A man reaps what he sows. The one who sows to please his sinful nature, from that nature will reap destruction; the one who sows to please the Spirit, from the Spirit will reap eternal life. Let us not become weary in doing good, for at the proper time we will reap a harvest if we do not give up.

As we yield to and sow love, for example, we will not only reap loving acts from others, but the powerful force of love will grow in us and make us better witnesses of Jesus. Through the power of the Holy Spirit and by yielding to His presence in us, we can lead fruitful, abundant lives!

The Holy Spirit Himself is at work in your students and will be a guiding hand as you teach these lessons. Trust Him to work through you as you explore the blessings of living a Spirit-directed life.

How to Use This Book

This book has nine lessons on each fruit of the Holy Spirit. Each lesson is based on a story from the Old Testament that demonstrates the Holy Spirit at work in people's lives. The supporting skits, play activities, and take-home assignments provide children with practical instruction on developing the fruit in their own lives.

Each lesson includes:
- A review of the previous lesson (starts with the second lesson)
- A scripture lesson with teaching tips and a paraphrase of the Scripture
- A skit about three modern-day children (Maggie, Jeffrey, and Peter) whose activities relate to those found in the Scripture lesson
- A hands-on play activity, art project, or game
- A take-home assignment sheet that informs parents about the lesson and provides an opportunity for real-life application of the fruit of the Spirit. It also includes a verse to memorize for the next class time. Scripture memory cards are on pages 46–47. Reproduce these to give each child a bookmark-sized copy of the verse for that lesson.

Depending on the time you have with students, you may choose to cover each lesson over one or two class times.

Time Estimates (times vary with class size and length of discussions)
- Review of take-home assignment: 5–15 minutes
- Review of memory verses: 10–15 minutes
- Lesson and paraphrase: 10–15 minutes
- Skit: 10 minutes
- Play activity: 15–30 minutes
- Take-home assignment sheet: 5 minutes (in class explanation)

Performing the Skits

Puppet and accessory patterns are included on page 48. Color the patterns or allow the children to color them. Cut out and then glue the characters to craft sticks. Tape the accessory pieces to the puppets when appropriate. Enlist the help of adults or older children to perform the skits for the class.

— the unfailing power of — # Love

The Fruit of Love

God's desire that we should love one another is so strong that Jesus deemed it one of the greatest commandments, second only to loving God Himself (see Matthew 22:37–40). The example of love that David and Jonathan modeled in their friendship is one that the children in your class will be able to relate to and incorporate into their lives.

David and Jonathan teach us about love in **1 Samuel 20:1–42**.
Read and discuss this passage with the children or use the paraphrase below.

David and Jonathan

David and Jonathan were best friends. Jonathan's father, King Saul, had been jealous of David ever since David had killed Goliath. David told Jonathan, "I think your father wants to hurt me." But Jonathan could not imagine how such a thing could be true. He told David that he would talk to his father to see if it were true.

The next day while Jonathan was eating dinner with his father, he found out that Saul not only wanted to hurt David, but that he was also mad at Jonathan for taking David's side. Jonathan slipped away and warned David about the danger to his life. Even though it meant that Jonathan's father would be mad at him and he might not ever see David again, Jonathan told David to run away and hide. Because Jonathan loved David, he thought that David's safety was more important than making his father happy and doing something wrong.

Play Ball

Jeffrey:	Hey, Peter. What should we do today?
Peter:	I want to play football.
Jeffrey:	Nope. How about soccer?
Peter:	No. Definitely football.
Jeffrey:	I'd much rather play soccer.
Peter:	You'll be playing football . . .
Jeffrey:	Soccer!
Peter:	Football!
Jeffrey:	Soccer!
Maggie:	What are you two arguing about?
Peter:	I want to play football. If Jeffrey were a real friend, he would play football with me.
Jeffrey:	And if Peter were a real friend, he would play soccer because that's what I want to do.
Maggie:	You're both wrong. Don't you remember the story about David and Jonathan? They were friends through thick and thin. It had nothing to do with them doing what the other one said they should. It's called love.
Jeffrey:	So, even when Peter doesn't want to play soccer with me, he's still my friend?
Maggie:	Yes.
Peter:	And even when Jeffrey won't play football with me, we're still friends?
Maggie:	That's right.
Peter:	We don't have to play football.
Jeffrey:	No, we don't have to play soccer.
Peter:	No, we don't have to play football!
Jeffrey:	I insist, we don't have to play soccer!
Maggie:	Here we go again!

Play Activity

Friendship Collage

This activity requires a stack of old magazines, large poster board, scissors, and glue. Have the children form groups of two or three. Give each group a piece of poster board with all of the group members' names written across the top. Tell them they are to pretend they have never met before. Instead of using words to introduce themselves, they must use pictures cut from the magazines and glued to the poster board.

Give the children plenty of time to work but save enough time to review the projects. Explain to the children that each piece of poster board now represents not each of them individually but a friendship that occurs when two or more people come together. There will be things they share in common but also plenty of individual interests. Just like David and Jonathan, they can still be friends—even with differences.

Take-Home Assignment

Explain to the children that the next time your class meets they will get to share one of their friendships with the class. Instruct the children to each bring in a photograph or other memento that represents a friend.

Copy page 9 for the children to take home. The note explains the lesson and enlists parent help in the completion of the assignment. It also contains a verse for the child to memorize for the next class time. You can also make each child a personal bookmark-sized copy of the verse from page 46.

— the unfailing power of — LOVE

But the fruit of the Spirit is LOVE, joy, peace, patience, kindness, goodness, faithfulness, gentleness and self-control.
(Galatians 5:22–23)

Name _____

Dear Parent:

In today's lesson, your child began learning about the fruit of the Spirit as described by Paul in his letter to the Galatians. Over the next months, our lessons will focus on each of the nine fruit of the Holy Spirit. Today, we discussed the first fruit—*love.* Our Bible lesson came from 1 Samuel 20:1–42. We learned how God blesses our lives by giving us loving friendships such as the one experienced by David and Jonathan. Your child teamed up with other children to create a collage that illustrated how people with different interests can still be friends.

For our next class, we would like each child to bring a picture or other memento that represents a friendship. The children will share this friendship with their classmates. If a photograph is not available, your child can draw a picture or choose another memento. For example, if the friend likes to roller skate, your child could bring in a picture of skates to tell about the friend.

God bless you,

_____

Please help your child learn the memory verse. The children will be given an opportunity to recite it at the beginning of our next class time together.
Memory verse:

Love one another.

John 13:34

— the strengthening
power of —

Joy

Review

Ask for volunteers to recite the memory verse: "Love one another." John 13:34
Reward memorizers with praise, stickers, or other small treats.

Give each child a chance to present her picture to the class. Encourage the children to share stories about their friends or qualities that makes their friends special.

The Fruit of Joy

King David had a passion for God. We can see it in the emotional Psalms he wrote that expressed both fear and confidence. We can see it in the moments of his life when he mustered courage to fight a giant or when he showed sorrow for his sins. Today's Scripture lesson is another example of David's heart for God. David demonstrates an unfettered joy at seeing the ark of the Covenant returned to Jerusalem. It is a joy that literally causes him to dance!

King David teaches us about joy in **2 Samuel 6:12–22**.
Read and discuss this passage with the children or use the paraphrase below.

David Dances for Joy

When David became king, everyone looked up to him. They thought he was a great leader and a very important man. He was, after all, the king.

But David knew there was something more important than being the king: being a child of God, just like *you* are. One day, the people were entering Jerusalem with the ark of the Covenant. This was a special box that contained the Ten Commandment tablets. And now the ark was coming to Jerusalem!

David was so full of joy that he began to dance in front of everyone. He did not care if he looked foolish; he was so happy about God!

When the ark was finally put in the tent that David had made for it, David gave offerings to God and food to all the people. His wife thought David acted like a fool. But David was simply acting like a joyous child of God.

Noise Makers

Peter: Hi, Maggie. What time is your family leaving for church?

Maggie: At nine. How about yours?

Peter: Same.

Maggie: You don't sound very excited.

Peter: I could be sleeping.

Maggie: Yeah, or playing. It's finally stopped raining.

Peter: Is there anyone who actually looks forward to church on Sunday?

Jeffrey: Can you guys believe it? Sunday again!

Peter: Yeah, we were just talking about it.

Jeffrey: Just think, we get to hear stories about God and sing songs . . .

Maggie: But we could be playing . . .

Peter: Sleeping . . .

Maggie Running around . . .

Peter: Making noise . . .

Jeffrey: We can make all the noise we want at church.

Maggie: What?

Jeffrey: The Bible tells us to make a joyful noise to the Lord. So, we pray and we sing. We say, "Thank you, God, for letting us play, sleep, and run around."

Maggie: Won't the grown-ups get mad?

Jeffrey: Nope. Because they are making noise, too. They're saying, "Thank you, God, for my family, for giving us everything we need, and for helping people."

Maggie: So, it's okay to make noise?

Jeffrey: Yep.

Peter: I'll race you guys to church.

Maggie: You're on!

Play Activity

Make a Joyful Noise!

This activity will work as a good starter (or refresher) course for children in the practice of praise and worship. Explain that what David was doing by dancing before the Lord is like what we do when we gather to worship the Lord in our churches today. Encourage children to dance before the Lord like King David did as they express joy for who He is and for what He has done.

Take a brief period to have the children brainstorm two things: attributes of God (strong, powerful, good, faithful, etc.) and things He has done for them (given them families, provided food, etc.). Make a list of the various ideas they provide.

Lead the children in a responsive reading based on Psalm 150. After saying the opening portion, point to one of the children for him to praise the Lord for something specific. Follow this model:

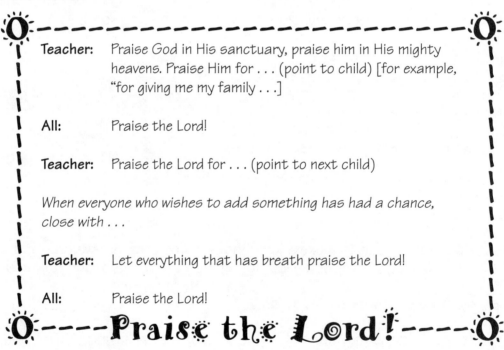

Teacher: Praise God in His sanctuary, praise him in His mighty heavens. Praise Him for . . . (point to child) [for example, "for giving me my family . . .]

All: Praise the Lord!

Teacher: Praise the Lord for . . . (point to next child)

When everyone who wishes to add something has had a chance, close with . . .

Teacher: Let everything that has breath praise the Lord!

All: Praise the Lord!

Praise the Lord!

Take-Home Assignment

Ask the children to find five things for which they are thankful and record them on a copy of page 14. The children should bring this sheet to the next class and then take it back home to post as a daily reminder of things for which they are thankful.

Copy page 13 for the children to take home. The note explains the lesson and enlists parent help in the completion of the assignment. It also contains a verse for the child to memorize for the next class time. You can also make each child a personal bookmark-sized copy of the verse from page 46.

— the strengthening
power of —
Joy

*But the fruit of the Spirit is love, JOY, peace,
patience, kindness, goodness, faithfulness,
gentleness and self-control.*
(Galatians 5:22–23)

Name _____

Dear Parent:

In today's lesson, your child learned about
the second fruit of the Spirit—*joy*. Our lesson
came from 2 Samuel 6:12–22. We learned
about the outrageous love of King David for
God, a love that caused him to literally dance
in the streets for joy, not caring who could see
him. Then, your child got a chance to join the
class in praising God for who He is and for
what He does for us.

Attached please find a sheet challenging your
child to find five things for which he or she
is thankful. Please help your child fill out this
form and return it to our next class to share
with the rest of the class. When it is brought
home again, please post it as a daily reminder
of the people, circumstances, and things that
God has given your child and that bring joy.

God bless you,

_____

Please help your child learn the memory verse. The children will be given
an opportunity to recite it at the beginning of our next class time together.

Memory verse:

"... the joy of the Lord is your strength."

Nehemiah 8:11

The Fruit of the Spirit: 1–3 • CD-2035

— the strengthening power of —

Joy

Name _____

God is so good!

When I look around, I see His world and the people and things He has given me. Thank You, God, for these gifts:

1. _____

2. _____

3. _____

4. _____

5. _____

— the protective power of — PEACE

Review

Ask for volunteers to recite the memory verse: ". . . the joy of the Lord is your strength." Nehemiah 8:11 Reward memorizers with praise, stickers, or other small treats.

Have each child share her praise sheet with the rest of the class. Encourage each child to take the sheet home and post it where she will see it every day.

The Fruit of Peace

The story of Noah and his ark is a great adventure story that all of the children in your class have probably heard. But did you know it can also make a great illustration for the fruit of the Spirit? God told Noah how to build the ark, even to the smallest detail. When the rains began accumulating into a flood that covered the earth, the only safe place left had to be in an ark of God's own design. Imagine the peace that Noah must have felt amid the turmoil. Today, this same peace is available to those who place their trust in God amid the storms of life.

Noah teaches us about peace in **Genesis 7:1–24**.
Read and discuss this passage with the children or use the paraphrase below.

Peace in a Storm

Dark clouds covered the earth. A big storm was brewing. Noah tried to tell everyone that the world would be flooded but no one believed him. In fact, they laughed at the big boat he was building. Noah looked at the rain clouds as he gathered his family, entered the boat, and led the animals two-by-two up the ramp into the belly of the great ship. How could he be sure this ship would even float?

Noah had faith in his boat because God had told him to build it, even telling him the smallest details. When everyone was inside, the Lord closed the door. As the rain began to collect into puddles on the ground, he pulled his family close. The boat began to groan and tip back and forth and then . . . it began to float!

For forty days and nights, the boat protected Noah and his family from the storm and from the flood. Noah had peace in his heart because he also had faith that God would protect him.

Safe at Home

Peter: Jeffrey! Come here! I need help!

Jeffrey: What's going on?

Peter: I'm building an ark, and I need someone to help me carry the wood.

Jeffrey: Why are you building an ark?

Peter: In case we get another flood. You heard the story about Noah in Sunday school today.

Jeffrey: Yeah, but Noah waited to build an ark until God told him to.

Peter: Well, it's never too soon to get started. If you help me, I will let you get on when the rain starts.

Jeffrey: It's a deal.

Maggie: Where are you guys going with all of that wood?

Peter: We're building an ark. You heard the story.

Maggie: But don't you remember . . . God told Noah that He would never flood the entire earth again. We don't need to build arks because we know that God will keep His promise.

Peter: Are you sure?

Maggie: Of course, I'm sure; God doesn't lie! God gave us parents to look out for us and a home to go to when it rains.

Jeffrey: I think she's got a point, Peter.

Maggie: What should we do with all this wood?

Peter: Remember the story of how King David had his son, Solomon, build the Temple in Jerusalem?

Maggie: You two get started. I'm going inside. It looks like rain.

Play Activity

Peace Time

The story of Noah and the ark illustrates resting peacefully in God's arms. When Noah left the ark, he worshipped God. Today, have the children worship God with their creativity. Make copies of the frame below for each child to draw a picture showing a

I have peace with God!

Take-Home Assignment

Ask the children about places in their homes where they can be alone with God. For this assignment, they will seek, like Noah, to create a peaceful place where they can go to worship Him. Suggest that each child keep the Bible in a place in her room that will be a personal worship space. Encourage them also to decorate their spaces as they see fit, starting with the pictures they created today.

Copy page 18 for each child to take home. The note explains the lesson and enlists parent help in the completion of the assignment. It also contains a verse for the child to memorize for the next class time. You can also make each child a personal bookmark-sized copy of the verse from page 46.

— the protective
power of —

Peace

But the fruit of the Spirit is love, joy, PEACE,
patience, kindness, goodness,
faithfulness, gentleness and self-control.
(Galatians 5:22–23)

Name _____

Dear Parent,

In today's class, your child learned about the third fruit of the Spirit—peace. Our lesson came from Genesis 7:1–24. We learned about the peace that God offers each of us in times of trouble. Noah was kept safe and sound from the flood that covered the earth. When he was finally able to leave his ark, Noah worshiped God. Today, your child was encouraged to create a personal worship space in your home. Help your child set up a place in his or her room for Bible reading, prayer, and worship. During our next class time, the children will be invited to tell the rest of the class about the spaces they created.

God bless you,

_____

Please help your child learn the memory verse. The children will be given an opportunity to recite it at the beginning of our next class time together.

Memory verse:

Let the peace of Christ rule in your hearts. . . .

Colossians 3:15

— the persevering power of — PATIENCE

(Before beginning the review, begin the Play Activity for this lesson. See page 21 for instructions.)

Review

Ask for volunteers to recite the memory verse: "Let the peace of Christ rule in your hearts. . . ." Colossians 3:15 Reward memorizers with praise, stickers, or other small treats.

Give each child an opportunity to discuss the worship space she made in her room. Ask about any special decorations she used.

The Fruit of Patience

Imagine being told that your greatest dream was about to come true. How long could you wait for it to happen? An hour? A week? A month? How about 25 years? That's how long Abraham waited between the time God told him he would have descendants and the moment at which he held his son for the first time. But Abraham knew that if God promised it, God would deliver it!

Abraham teaches us about patience in **Genesis 12:1–6 and 21:1–7**.
Read and discuss this passage with the children or use the paraphrase below.

Abraham and Patience

Abram and Sarai were a happy couple. They had everything they wanted.

Everything but a child, that is. How they wanted to have a baby! One day, God told Abram that he would be the father of a nation. Of course, this also meant that he would be the father of a child. Abram was so excited. What good news! Abram knew that if God said it would happen, it would happen.

So Abram and Sarai waited. And they waited. And they waited some more. The years came and went. By the time Abram was about to turn 100 years old, God had changed Abram's name to Abraham and Sarai's name to Sarah. Abraham was visited by three men sent by God, who told him he was about to become a father. Sarah laughed because she had heard that one before. But Abraham knew that if God said it would happen, it would happen.

One year later Sarah gave birth to a baby boy. She named him Isaac, because it meant "laughter." But Abraham didn't laugh because he knew that if God said it would happen, it would happen. And guess what . . . it happened!

Waiting

Maggie: Hi Peter, what are you doing?

Peter: I'm waiting.

Maggie: For what?

Peter: To grow up.

Maggie: That could take forever. What's the hurry?

Peter: Grown-ups get all the fun. They get to drive; they get to have jobs . . .

Maggie: Own a house . . .

Peter: Travel to foreign countries . . .

Maggie: Vote . . .

Peter: Not just vote . . . they can be president!

Maggie: They can do what they want . . .

Peter: Wear what they want . . .

Maggie: Eat what they want . . .

Peter: When they want . . .

Maggie: On whatever furniture they want . . .

Peter: Until they go to bed. At whatever time they want.

Maggie: Wow. Do you mind if I wait with you?

Jeffrey: Hey, guess what I just remembered. We have a month of summer vacation left . . . No school for a whole month . . . no worries . . . no homework . . . no getting up early. Nothing but free time. Isn't it great being a kid?

Maggie: You know, God looks after us little guys, too!

Play Activity

Hold Your Cookies
Begin this play activity at the start of the lesson. As the children enter the room, give each child a cookie. Tell them not to eat the cookies until after they get through the Memory Verse and Review portions of the class. Once these portions are over, tell them to wait until after the Bible lesson is over. When the Bible lesson is over, ask them how they would feel if they had to wait until the very end of the class to eat their cookies. As you discuss their answers, remind the children that as we exercise the patience that God has placed in us, we will grow stronger in this area. When we exercise patience and wait to enjoy the blessings of God in His timing, they will be even sweeter.

Take-Home Assignment
Before class, write each child's name on an envelope and seal a piece of candy inside. Give the envelopes to the children as they leave and instruct them to bring them to the next class time, at which time they will be allowed to open them. The children will be learning about the patience involved in living in anticipation.

— the persevering power of — # Patience

Name _____

But the fruit of the Spirit is love, joy, peace, PATIENCE, kindness, goodness, faithfulness, gentleness and self-control.
(Galatians 5:22–23)

Dear Parent:

In today's lesson, your child learned about the fourth fruit of the Spirit—*patience.* Our lesson came from Genesis 12:1–6 and 21:1–7. We learned about the patience of Abraham as he waited for God to fulfill the promise He made to give him descendants. In class, we played a patience game, and now I would appreciate your help in playing one more. Inside the envelope your child brought home is a treat. Your child has been asked not to open the envelope until he or she returns to class. Please keep this envelope in plain sight and when the opportunity arises, discuss the difficulty of waiting for a surprise. Be sure to send the envelope back with your child to our next class time

God bless

_____

Please help your child learn the memory verse. The children will be given an opportunity to recite it at the beginning of our next class time together.

Memory verse:

. . . be patient with everyone.

1 Thessalonians 5:14

— the power to be a blessing — KINDNESS

Review

Ask for volunteers to recite the memory verse: ". . . be patient with everyone."
1 Thessalonians 5:14 Reward memorizers with praise, stickers, or other small treats.

Before allowing the children to open the envelopes, ask them if it was difficult to wait to find out what was in the envelope. Remind the children of the value of patience and allow them to enjoy the candy.

The Fruit of Kindness

Some people assume that the Old Testament is just a book of big adventures and loud prophets. Sure, it has both of those, but in stories like Ruth, we also find sublime moments of love, tenderness, and kindness. Especially notable are the acts of Boaz to ensure the comfort and sustenance of distant relatives he barely knew. He models for us the kindness we can show through the power of the Holy Spirit not only to people we know but to our brothers and sisters the world over.

Boaz teaches us about kindness in **Ruth 2**.
Read and discuss this chapter with the children or use the paraphrase below.

The Kindness of Boaz

Ruth and Naomi were poor and hungry. They did not know where their next meal would come from. Naomi had an idea. She told Ruth to go to a field where some people were harvesting grain. She said that if she walked behind them in the field, she could pick up the scraps they left behind, and they could make barley bread.

Ruth did as Naomi told her and went to the field and began picking up the grain the harvesters left behind. The owner of the field was a man named Boaz, and when he saw Ruth picking the grain, he allowed her to eat lunch with the other workers. He told some of the workers to even purposely drop extra grain so that Ruth would be able to pick up more.

That night Ruth went home and surprised Naomi with big armfuls of grain she had picked from the field. That had plenty of food, and they were thankful for the kindness of Boaz.

The Lost Money

Peter: Look, a twenty-dollar bill!

Maggie: Whose is it?

Peter: I don't know. It was just lying here on the ground.

Jeffrey: We should find who it belongs to and return it . . .

Maggie: It could belong to anyone, Jeffrey. This is a busy street.

Peter: Twenty dollars! That's practically a fortune. We could buy anything we want!

Jeffrey: Someone might be looking for it. He might need it to buy food.

Maggie: There's nothing we can do about it.

Peter: Are you kidding? It's twenty dollars! We can get ice cream every day!

Jeffrey: We could go door to door asking people if they lost it. They might
             need it for paying rent.

Maggie: We can't go to everyone's door asking them if they lost money!

Jeffrey: It might be money they need for medicine. We could see if someone's name
             is written on it.

Maggie: There is . . . his name is Andrew Jackson, silly.

Jeffrey: Wait a second . . . Was it folded in the shape of a triangle?

Peter: Yes, it was.

Jeffrey: Then, it must be mine! I lost it this morning and I fold all my big bills
             like that.

Maggie: Why do you do that?

Jeffrey: If I didn't, how would you guys have been able to return it to me? Thanks!
             Anybody want ice cream?

Maggie: Yes, I would! That's very kind of you, Jeffrey!

Play Activity

I Love You Because . . .

Boaz showed love for distant relatives. Have each of the children pick a relative and prepare a card or letter for the relative with the theme "I love you because . . ." Explain to the children that even more valuable than the food Boaz provided was the love that he showed to Naomi and Ruth. Even though the children in your class might not have material things to share at their age, they do have an infinite amount of love. Point out this asset to them.

Take-Home Assignment

Instruct the children to deliver or send their cards or letters to the persons for whom they made them.

Copy page 26 for children to take home. This note explains the lesson and enlists parent help in the completion of the assignment. It also contains a verse for the child to memorize for the next class time. You can also make each child a personal bookmark-sized copy of the verse from page 46.

— the power to be a blessing —

Kindness

But the fruit of the Spirit is love, joy, peace, patience, KINDNESS, goodness, faithfulness, gentleness and self-control.
(Galatians 5:22–23)

Name _____

Dear Parent:

In today's class, your child learned about the fifth fruit of the Spirit—*kindness*. Our lesson came from Ruth 2. We learned about the love that Boaz showed for his distant relatives Ruth and Naomi. Your child has prepared a card or letter for a family member with whom he or she would like to share love. Please help by passing this token of love along to the person for whom it was intended. Share any response you receive with your child.

God bless you,

Please help your child learn the memory verse. The children will be given an opportunity to recite it at the beginning of our next class time together.

Memory verse:

. . . be kind to each other . . . .

1 Thessalonians 5:15

26

— the overcoming power of —

Goodness

Review

Ask for volunteers to recite the memory verse: ". . . be kind to each other. . . ."
1 Thessalonians 5:15 Have the children tell about the feedback they received from the recipients of their cards or letters.

The Fruit of Goodness

Goodness is not something we do, it is something we are because of the Holy Spirit in us. As Jesus said, "There is only One who is good." (Matthew 19:17) Goodness is a quality that God builds into us, just as He built it into all creation!

The Lord shows us what goodness is all about it in **Genesis 1**.
Read and discuss this chapter with the children or use the paraphrase below.

The Goodness of the Lord

In the beginning, God made heaven. He also made the earth. He made light. He made day and night. He made water and dry land. He made plants and trees. God made animals on the ground and in the sky and in the sea. And then, He made people like you and me.

Every time God made something new, He looked at it and said the same thing: "It is good." God did not create anything that was bad, broken, or wrong. Everything God made was good. And that includes *you*!

The Poll

Maggie: Hey guys. I'm taking a poll for my Sunday school class.

Peter: A what?

Maggie: A poll. I ask people what they are happy that God created, and then I write down what they say.

Jeffrey: I'll start. I'm happy God created rain . . .

Peter: Are you kidding? Rain gets you wet . . .

Maggie: It also makes farm crops grow . . .

Peter: It makes soccer games get cancelled . . .

Maggie: It fills the lakes so we can go for boat rides or fish off of a dock . . .

Peter: It means we can't go out during recess . . .

Maggie: It causes trees and plants to grow . . .

Peter: It makes me have to mow the lawn more often . . .

Maggie: It leaves a rainbow when it is gone . . .

Peter: It makes me have to leave my muddy shoes outside . . .

Maggie: Why do you like the rain, Jeffrey?

Jeffrey: It makes popcorn.

Maggie: You mean it causes corn to grow, which, once it is harvested, can be taken off the cob and then sold as popcorn kernels that you can buy and pop to make popcorn?

Jeffrey: No. Because when it rains, my mom makes me clean my room, and if I do a good job, she makes popcorn. We get to sit and have popcorn together in the middle of the day, for no good reason.

Peter: How is your poll going Maggie?

Maggie: Very slowly.

Jeffrey: Did I mention how glad I am that God created snow?

Play Activity

It's All Good

On a chalkboard or a piece of poster board, write the words "God Created." Then, tell the children that for the next few minutes they should name things that are good. Record the words they offer and discuss which of the things on the list God created. Of course, the answer is "everything." Explain that anything good that they can think of came from God's hands.

Take-Home Assignment

Have the children discover more "good things" in their homes. Send a copy of page 31 home with each child. Instruct them to record good things related to their homes or families and to bring the papers back to the next class time.

Copy page 30 for the children to take home. This note explains the lesson and enlists parent help in the completion of the assignment. It also contains a verse for the child to memorize for the next class time. You can also make each child a personal bookmark-sized copy of the verse from page 47.

— the overcoming power of — Goodness

But the fruit of the Spirit is love, joy, peace, patience, kindness, GOODNESS, faithfulness, gentleness and self-control."
(Galatians 5:22–23)

Name _____

Dear Parent:

In today's class, your child learned about the sixth fruit of the Spirit—*goodness*. Our lesson came from Genesis 1. We learned that God is the source of all goodness. Anything termed "good" can be done so because God created it. In class, we made a list of "good things." Please help your child find three "good things" in your home or neighborhood, list them on the attached sheet, and return it with him or her to our next class.

God bless you,

_____

Please help your child learn the memory verse. The children will be given an opportunity to recite it at the beginning of our next class time together.

Memory verse:

. . . overcome evil with good.

Romans 12:21

Name _____

In the beginning God created . . .

1. _____

2. _____

3. _____

. . . and it was ALL Good!

(Genesis 1:31)

The Fruit of the Spirit: 1–3 • CD-2035

Faithfulness
— the power that brings blessings —

Review

Ask for volunteers to recite the memory verse: ". . . overcome evil with good." Romans 12:21 Allow the children to share their "good things" lists with the class. Praise the Lord together for the different ways that He has shown His goodness to the children.

The Fruit of Faithfulness

We can rely on God for everything: to keep His word, to provide for us, and to guide and keep us. Being in a close relationship with God provides us with the distinct privilege of being able to say that God relies on us as well. God uses us to care for His people and His world, and He loves it so much when we worship Him. In today's lesson, Daniel demonstrates his faithfulness to God even when prayer is forbidden by earthly rulers.

Daniel teaches us about faithfulness in **Daniel 6:1–23**.
Read and discuss this passage with the children or use the paraphrase below.

Daniel: Faithful in Prayer

Daniel was a leader in Babylon. The other leaders were jealous of what a good job he did, and they planned to get him into trouble. They told the king to pass a law that people could only worship him. The men knew Daniel would only worship God.

After the law was passed, they waited until Daniel was praying to God. This was not hard because Daniel prayed to God three times a day. They told the king that Daniel was breaking the law and must be punished by spending a night in a den of lions—hungry lions. The king liked Daniel but the law was the law, after all. He was afraid for Daniel because the king knew that the lions would probably kill Daniel.

The next morning, the king rushed to the lions' den hoping that Daniel was still alive. What a surprise, there Daniel sat with the lions and not a scratch on him! Daniel said, "God protected me because He knew I did nothing wrong!" The king was so happy!

Remember to Not Forget

Peter: Hey, Maggie, what time is it?

Maggie: It's 1:00.

Peter: Jeffrey said to be here at 1:00, where is he?

Maggie: Give him time; give him time.

Peter: Here he comes. Hey, Jeffrey, what's with making us wait?

Jeffrey: I apologize, guys. I was praying.

Peter: In the middle of the day?

Maggie: Sure Peter, you can pray whenever you want.

Peter: But we have important plans . . .

Maggie: What are we doing anyway?

Peter: I don't know. Just hanging out.

Jeffrey: I told God I'd hang out with Him every day by praying after I eat my lunch.

Maggie: That's a good idea, Jeffrey.

Peter: Yeah, but can't you just "forget" once in a while? God won't mind.

Jeffrey: Maybe not, but when I pray I am saying "thank you" for so many things that He has remembered to do for me, that I would feel bad if I just "forgot."

Maggie: That's right. Nothing should keep us from talking to God every day.

Peter: I just store it up in my head and talk to him at night.

Maggie: What if you forget?

Peter: I *never* forget. In fact, tonight I'm going to tell him thank you for . . . no wait, I'm going to ask him to help me . . . umm . . .

Maggie: You never forget?

Peter: I'd better pray right now!

Jeffrey: Take your time. We'll wait.

Play Activity

Create a "Daniel Prayer"

Daniel showed his faithfulness by continuing to pray to God even when praying was outlawed. This project will give the children in your class a reminder of the story and its lesson. Ask the children to put a prayer in writing. Remind the children that they can talk to God just like they would talk to their closest friends. Suggest that they can begin by thanking God for being with them through the day and talk with Him about all their needs and concerns. Have the children write their prayers on copies of page 35.

Take-Home Assignment

Have the children take their "Daniel Prayers" home and put them in their worship spaces. Copy page 36 for the children to take home. This note explains the lesson and enlists parent help in the completion of the assignment. It also contains a verse for the child to memorize for the next class time. You can also make each child a personal bookmark-sized copy of the verse from page 47.

My "Daniel Prayer"

Name _____

"Now when Daniel learned that the decree had been published, he went home to his upstairs room where the windows opened toward Jerusalem. Three times a day he got down on his knees and prayed, giving thanks to his God, just as he had done before." Daniel 6:10

My prayer is:

_____

_____

_____

_____

_____

Evening, morning and noon . . .
he hears my voice.

Psalm 55:17

— the power that brings blessings — Faithfulness

But the fruit of the Spirit is love, joy, peace, patience, kindness, goodness, FAITHFULNESS, gentleness and self-control.
(Galatians 5:22–23)

Name _____

Dear Parent:

In today's class, your child learned about the seventh fruit of the Spirit—*faithfulness*. Our lesson came from Daniel 6:1–23. We learned about Daniel, who showed his faithfulness by facing a lions' den instead of refusing to pray to God. Your child has prepared a "Daniel Prayer" for the worship space you helped prepare a few weeks ago when we studied Noah. Please help your child to find a place there to display this prayer.

God bless you,

_____

Please help your child learn the memory verse. The children will be given an opportunity to recite it at the beginning of our next class time together.

Memory verse:

A faithful man will be richly blessed. . . .

Proverbs 28:20

— the power to
turn things around —

Gentleness

Review

Ask volunteers to recite the memory verse: "A faithful man will be richly blessed."
Proverbs 28:20. Have the children discuss what they did with their "Daniel Prayers." Where did
they place them? How have they used them?

The Fruit of Gentleness

Jesus asked "What good is it for a man to gain the whole world, yet forfeit his soul?"
Mark 8:36. In today's lesson, we see gentleness embodied in a man who is given
great power but exercises great compassion. The story of Joseph's reunion with the brothers
who sold him into slavery is an excellent example in forgiveness, love, and, of course,
gentleness.

Joseph teaches us about gentleness in **Genesis 45:1–15**.
Read and discuss this passage with the children or use the paraphrase below.

A Great Gentleness

Joseph's brothers were in trouble. They had gone to Egypt to get food and now
were being accused of stealing, and someone was going to have to go to prison.
Their father was still mourning their long-lost brother Joseph and could not bear
to lose another son.

The man in charge looked sternly at Joseph's brothers. They wondered how the
situation could get any worse. The man surprised them when he said: "I am your
brother Joseph—the one you sold into slavery. I ended up in prison for many
years, but now I have become an important person in Egypt." The brothers waited
for Joseph to tell them what he was going to do to them to get revenge for the
bad way they had treated him. Would he beat them? Would he throw them all
into prison?

Joseph stepped forward and hugged them. He cried because he was so happy
to be with his brothers. He explained to them that God had made it possible for
them all to have food to eat and a place to live.

The Fruit of the Spirit: 1–3 • CD-2035

The Lemonade Stand

Peter: Step right up, step right up! Homemade lemonade, ten cents a glass.

Jeffrey: Ice-cold lemonade!

Maggie: Hey guys!

Peter: No time to talk, we have to move some lemonade here!

Maggie: I'd love some lemonade! How much?

Peter: Ten cents a glass . . .

Jeffrey: But since you are a friend . . .

Peter: TEN CENTS A GLASS!

Maggie: Okay, well let's see . . . oh no, there's a hole in the bottom of my purse. Oh no, all of my money fell out. And my gum. And my acorn collection!

Peter: No money?

Maggie: No.

Peter: Gum?

Maggie: No.

Jeffrey: Acorns?

Maggie: No.

Peter: Move it along. No pay, no play. We're not a charity . . .

Jeffrey: But Peter, Maggie just lost everything in her purse . . .

Maggie: Well, I have a tissue . . .

Jeffrey: Since we are her friends, maybe we could be nice to her and give her some lemonade . . .

Peter: For free? That's crazy . . .

Jeffrey: Maybe . . . but I think it might be the right thing to do. Remember how Joseph knew that the right thing to do was to be kind to his brothers? And Maggie didn't even sell us to Egypt like Joseph's brothers did to him.

Peter: You're right! Have an extra large glass of lemonade, Maggie!

Play Activity

Learning Gentleness with Plants

One way gentleness is demonstrated is in the way we nurture or care for others. This exercise will give the children in your class an opportunity to exercise this value in a practical, measurable way. Before class, obtain a small plant or seedling for each child. Find blank labels that will fit on the sides of the planters. During class, have each child write "The fruit of the Spirit is . . . gentleness." on a label and place it on the side of each planter. Be sure to give them instructions on how to check whether the plants need water (depending on the particular plant you have chosen). Explain that just as Joseph cared for his brothers and gave them a place to live and food to eat, they will be caring for these plants.

Take-Home Assignment

Send the plants home with the children. Have them ask their parents for help finding a place to put them. Copy page 40 for the children to take home. This note explains the lesson and enlists parent help in the completion of the assignment. It also contains a verse for the child to memorize for the next class time. You can also make each child a personal bookmark-sized copy of the verse from page 47.

Gentleness

— the power to turn things around —

But the fruit of the Spirit is love, joy, peace, patience, kindness, goodness, faithfulness, GENTLENESS and self-control.
(Galatians 5:22–23)

Name _____

Dear Parent:

In today's class, your child learned about the eighth fruit of the Spirit—*gentleness*. Our Bible lesson came from Genesis 45:1–15. We saw the gentleness that Joseph demonstrated toward his brothers when he forgave them and provided food and a place for them to live. Today, each child is bringing home a plant to care for. Please help your child find an appropriate place in your home for this plant and assist in caring for it.

God bless you,

_____

Please help your child learn the memory verse. The children will be given an opportunity to recite it at the beginning of our next class time together.

Memory verse:

A gentle answer turns away wrath....

Proverbs 15:1

— the enabling power of — Self-Control

Review

Ask for volunteers to recite the memory verse: "A gentle answer turns away wrath."
Proverbs 15:1 Have the children share where they put their plants and give updates on how they are caring for them.

The Fruit of Self-Control

The term "self-control" is unusual because it implies something that people initiate for themselves. In reality, any such strength that we term "self-control" comes to us from God. Thus, self-control is very much a fruit of the Spirit. As we exercise the self-control that God has placed in us, it grows and develops.

The Lord used manna to teach us about self-control in **Exodus 16:4–30**.
Read and discuss this passage with the children or use the paraphrase below.

Manna in the Desert

After God freed the Israelites from slavery in Egypt, they traveled through the desert in search of their new homeland. Even though God Himself guided them, they began to worry and think that they had been forgotten. They really began to worry when they got hungry.

"How will we ever get food?" they asked Moses. But Moses knew God would provide for them. Moses was right, for God told him to tell the people that every day he would provide meat and bread for the people right in front of their tents. The one thing they needed to do was show that they trusted God by taking only enough food for one day at a time.

On the first day that the food appeared, people could not control themselves. They gathered up as much food as they could, more than enough for one day. They next morning, instead of looking for the food God provided outside, they went to the food they had stocked up and found that it was spoiled.

Starting the next day, they began trusting God and controlling how much food they took, and God provided for them the whole time they were on their journey.

Running in Circles

Maggie: Why is Peter running around in circles?

Jeffrey: He asked his mother if he could watch television, and she said that it was more important for him to get out every day and exercise.

Maggie: Well, it is. But that doesn't explain why he is just going round and round. Hey, Peter, come here!

Peter: (Huffing and puffing) I can't, must keep running. Round and round . . .

Maggie: But why?

Peter: No time to talk. You tell her Jeffrey . . .

Jeffrey: Okay. Peter figured out that if he does all of his exercise for a month at one time, then he can stay in for a whole month and watch television.

Maggie: That's ridiculous! You can't store up exercise for a month. Not even for a week. Hey, Peter, come here!

Peter: (Still huffing and puffing) Now what?

Maggie: Peter, you need to trust that God will give you all the time you need for the important things in life.

Peter: After I exercise!

Maggie: But your body needs rest, too. It's like food and water. Your body needs them both.

Peter: My body needs television! (continues running)

Jeffrey: How will his body tell him it needs rest?

Maggie: It will send him mysterious little signals . . .

Peter: Owww!

Maggie: . . . like making him so tired he runs into that tree!

Play Activity

Slow and Steady

Before class, obtain about 10 table tennis balls. Other types of balls will work, but table tennis balls work best for little hands. Bring an empty coffee can or other container. Have each child take a turn at seeing how many balls he can pick up in one minute. The trick is, children cannot put the balls anywhere; they must keep them in their hands.

When everyone has had an opportunity to try this, challenge them to see how many balls they can pick up in 30 seconds, but this time they are to pick up the balls only one at a time and then place them in a coffee can. At the end of thirty seconds, they will probably have more balls in the can than they did in their hands when they had a whole minute. Explain to them how self-control does more to help than it does to hinder. Having guidelines and a place to put the balls is actually easier than playing in a frenzy without any rules.

Take-Home Assignment

Copy pages 44 and 45 for the children to take home. Page 44 contains a riddle about each fruit of the Spirit. Page 45 thanks the parents for their involvement in the lessons that introduced their children to the fruit of the Spirit. It also contains a verse for the child to memorize for the next class time. Challenge students to also memorize Galatians 5:22-23, where the fruit of the Spirit are listed. You can also make each child a personal bookmark-sized copy of the verses from page 47.

Answers to Fruit of the Spirit Riddles, page 44: love, self-control, faithfulness, kindness, patience, gentleness, peace, goodness, joy.

The Fruit of the Spirit: 1–3 • CD-2035

Fruit of the Spirit Riddles

Name _____

God Himself is this fruit of the Spirit. It is the most powerful force in the universe. It causes all the other fruit to be productive. It never grows weak, and it never fails! **Which fruit is it?** _____ Clue: 1 John 4:16	Another word for this fruit of the Spirit is discipline. It helps you to put God first and to pray. Proverbs tells us that it's better to have this fruit than to be in charge of a whole city! **Which fruit is it?** _____ Clue: 1 Peter 4:7	When you practice this fruit of the Spirit, people will know they can depend on you. Growing in this fruit brings rich blessings to you! **Which fruit is it?** _____ Clue: Proverbs 28:20
When you practice this fruit of the Spirit, you won't try to get people back when you are mistreated. You'll always be ready to help others with actions and words! **Which fruit is it?** _____ Clue: 1 Thessalonians 5:15	This fruit of the Spirit helps you not to give up in difficult situations. Team this fruit with faith and you can receive what God has promised you! **Which fruit is it?** _____ Clue: Hebrews 6:12	This fruit of the Spirit gives you power not to be harsh or rude. It helps you show respect to others. Exercise this fruit and watch an angry person become calm! **Which fruit is it?** _____ Clue: Proverbs 15:1
Listening and watching for this fruit of the Spirit and allowing it to rule in your heart will help you make decisions. It protects your heart and mind and goes beyond what you can understand! **Which fruit is it?** _____ Clue: Philippians 4:7	This fruit of the Spirit can overcome any evil. When you practice this fruit with your enemies, God has promised you a great reward! **Which fruit is it?** _____ Clue: Romans 12:21	This fruit of the Spirit gives you supernatural strength! It is different from happiness. Happiness depends on what is happening, but you can have this fruit all the time—it comes from being in the Lord's presence! **Which fruit is it?** _____ Clue: Psalm 16:11

— the enabling power of — Self-Control

But the fruit of the Spirit is love, joy, peace, patience, kindness, goodness, faithfulness, gentleness and SELF-CONTROL.
(Galatians 5:22–23)

Name _____

Dear Parent:

In today's class, your child learned about the ninth fruit of the Spirit—*self-control.* Our lesson came from Exodus 16:4–30. We learned about the self-control the Israelites had to exercise in the desert when God told them to take only the food they needed for one day and how this caused the Israelites to learn to trust and rely on God. To review each fruit of the Spirit, assist your child in completing the attached riddles.

I now invite you to begin (or continue) an ongoing dialogue with your child regarding what it means to live day-by-day relying on and trusting God.

Thank you for all of your help as your child studied the fruit of the Spirit!

God bless you,

_____

Please help your child learn the memory verses. The children will be given an opportunity to recite them at the beginning of our next class time together.

Memory verses:

Like a city whose walls are broken down is a man who lacks self-control.
Proverbs 25:28

But the fruit of the Spirit is love, joy, peace, patience, kindness, goodness, faithfulness, gentleness and self-control.
Galatians 5:22–23

Love one another.

John 13:34

"... the joy of the Lord is your strength."

Nehemiah 8:10

Let the peace of Christ rule in your hearts. ...

Colossians 3:15

...be patient with everyone.

1 Thessalonians 5:14

...be kind to each other ....

1 Thessalonians 5:15

... overcome evil with good.

Romans 12:21

A faithful man
will be richly blessed. . . .

Proverbs 28:20

A gentle answer turns
away wrath . . . .

Proverbs 15:1

Like a city whose walls are
broken down is a man
who lacks self-control.

Proverbs 25:28

But the fruit of the Spirit is love, joy,
peace, patience, kindness, goodness,
faithfulness, gentleness and self-control.

Galatians 5:22–23

The Fruit of the Spirit: 1–3 • CD-2035

Puppets and accessories to use with skits
Color the puppets and accessory pieces.
Cut out and glue them to craft sticks.
Tape the accessory pieces to the puppets when appropriate.

soccer ball
(use with p.7)

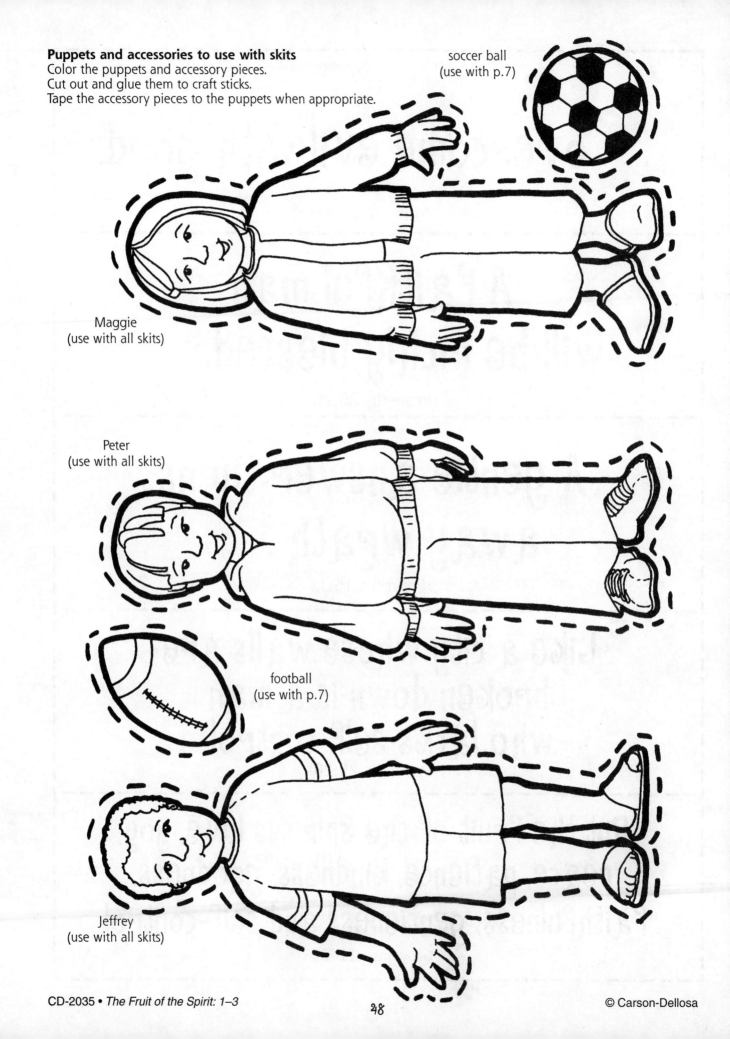

Maggie
(use with all skits)

Peter
(use with all skits)

football
(use with p.7)

Jeffrey
(use with all skits)